Time Management

Leverage The Strength Of Time Management Science To Scientifically Conquer Procrastination

(Techniques And Strategies To Overcome Laziness And Stop Procrastination)

Stefan Ashworth

TABLE OF CONTENT

Introduction 1

Chapter 1: Create A Support Network Of Acquaintances And Family Members. 3

Chapter 2: Prioritizing Organizational Priorities Is Essential.. 6

Chapter 3: Techniques For Instructing Youth In Time Management.. 9

Chapter 4: The Productivity Strategy That Saved My Life 15

Chapter 5: How Developing Positive Habits............23

Chapter 6: The Advantages Of Effective Time Management 27

Chapter 7: Why Effective Time Management Is Crucial..50

Chapter 8: Time Management: What Is It? 57

Chapter 9: The Day As It Actually Occurs 65

Chapter 10: Beginning With Module One 69

Chapter 11: The Workings Of Time Management.78

Chapter 12: The Adverse Effects Of Procrastination 81

Chapter 13: Replace The Slave Insect..........................87

Chapter 14: Commence The Day Properly................94

Chapter 15: Ineffective Is A Long To-Do List........108

Chapter 16: Our Most Valuable Currency Must Be Time..122

Chapter 17: Overcoming Dependencies / Conquering Dependencies..133

Chapter 18: Time Management Skills......................145

Chapter 19: Why Do We Delayed Action?...............151

Chapter 20: The Importance Of Time Administration..154

Conclusion...159

Introduction

Let me begin by expressing my admiration for all the strong mothers out there, and then share some time management techniques I've developed over the years in my endeavors to raise money for my business while simultaneously raising a family.

Parenting is one of the many responsibilities that accompany great authority. That's double the stress if you're raising your children alone and operating a business at the same time.

One out of every three children in the United States is raised by a single parent; therefore, it is imperative that we debate these issues and find solutions for working women.

Raising a child alone is a difficult experience. As a single mother, you are exclusively responsible for the daily care of your children. If you are a single working mother struggling to find time for yourself, you are not alone. Being a single mother can result in stress, exhaustion, and heightened pressure. There is never enough time in a day to accomplish everything one desires. There is not enough time to accomplish everything on the growing number of to-do lists. When the list of tasks grows lengthier, you may feel overwhelmed and procrastinate.

The time management of single mothers differs greatly from that of married mothers. As long as you are on your own, responsibilities can continue.

Chapter 1: Create A Support Network Of Acquaintances And Family Members.

Single mothers can rely on a network of acquaintances and family members, as well as neighbors, for assistance when they need it. If someone offers you assistance, take it without hesitation.

Set some ground principles

Be clear with those you rely on for assistance with child care, grocery purchasing, homework, and the like. Set a reasonable and responsible amount that you anticipate requesting, so that your helper does not feel uncomfortable assisting you when your needs are unmet.

Avoid requesting rent, bills, or other financial assistance from companions. Accept financial assistance for child care or sustenance if offered. Even if they cannot pay, you should not take it personally. When you request assistance from a loved one, be gracious and say "thank you" if they offer to assist.

Set a positive example

If your needs are not being met because your spouse or companion is frequently absent, make it a priority to set a good example for your children. Spend significant time with them. Provide them with as much love and affection as you can. Let them know that you will be there for them while their father is abroad.

Be willing to aid.

The proverb "it takes a village to raise a child" applies to single parents. You're not alone. You simply need to know where to go when your demands are unmet. Do not squander valuable energy worrying about things outside of your control. Take charge and parent responsibly.

Look after yourself

No one else can assist your children emotionally and physically if you cannot. Parent while remaining healthful. The more time and effort you devote to self-care, the better parent you will be.

Chapter 2: Prioritizing Organizational Priorities Is Essential.

Determine and implement an effective organizing system. Use your phone's calendar or notes app to keep track of your tasks and appointments. Review your schedule weekly to determine if you will need to contact your support network at any point during the week.

Each week, I schedule a certain quantity of time away from the children. Approximately twelve hours per week. On most weekends, I spend the day after school drop-off at a friend's house, and then I collect up the children after school. I'll have the children from Thursday evening to Monday evening for a week-long weekend. Evenings are spent either playing a family game (such as charades or Battleship) or spending quality time together. If the weather permits, we will visit the park.

We are repeatedly told that mothers must be available 24/7. It's utter nonsense. We do not need to be constantly accessible. We must establish limits for what we can reasonably handle.

Consider your physical limitations with realism

Consider your body and how it reacts to your offspring with realism. There will be times when you will need a quick energy snack in order to keep up with your children and maintain a conversation with your peers. You will have no time to unwind after a long day. You will need to establish and adhere to your limits. You're not doing it correctly if you're constantly on the precipice of tears.

Practice saying no, and then don't be afraid to state it when necessary.

We have always said "yes" to our children's requests, regardless of whether we had the energy, time, or motivation to provide the expected level of attention and care. We're simply not good at setting limits, so we set "yes" as the default and become inundated by the results.

Chapter 3: Techniques For Instructing Youth In Time Management

Most individuals struggle to effectively manage their time. Rarely are adolescents an exception. Academic, social, athletic, volunteer, and familial responsibilities are just a few of the constraints on their leisure time. How can we then assist adolescents in learning to prioritize their duties and effectively manage their time? Parents may be a valuable resource if they intervene and provide advice.

You will be able to offer advice to reduce your teen's tension once you have gained an understanding of the various aspects of time management for adolescents.

Seven Methods to Teach Youth Time Management

1. Determine Your Teen's Style
Begin by assisting your adolescent to recognize her unique rhythms. There are times during the day when everyone is more productive than at other times. It is more beneficial for parents to assist children in identifying their productive periods than to dictate what they should be doing at what times. Providing autonomy to adolescents is essential for efficient time management.

2. Discuss Stress Management Techniques

Because they can be so overwhelming, high levels of tension inhibit effective time management. The two primary categories of stress are internal and external. Individuals generate their own internal tension ("I need straight As!"). Stress is caused by deadlines and other external demands, such as "I have a math exam tomorrow!" If your child is under excessive external pressure, attempt to alleviate it by delaying the start of projects and other responsibilities, requesting more time from teachers, or discontinuing extracurricular activities. If your adolescent tends to place a great deal of internal strain on himself, look for ways to help him maintain a healthy perspective on what is essential (and what is not).

3. Teach Your Teenage Child About Priorities "I have an important math

exam on Monday morning, but all of my pals are going to the movies on Sunday night. Could I join you? Teenagers, whose minds have not yet developed the capacity to perceive consequences, may not view this remark as problematic, despite the fact that most adults would. By discussing priorities, such as obtaining a B in arithmetic, with their children, parents can help their children become better time managers. To earn the B you've mentioned, you must perform well on your exam. Would you be able to study in the afternoon so that you could complete the exam before the movie?

4. Commence Your Day Early
Indicators of procrastination and poor time management include arriving late to events, failing to complete assignments by the deadline, and

delaying preparations for a family gathering until the last minute. When parents observe that their children's behavior is negatively impacting their grades and causing conflict, they must intervene and teach them how to complete homework and other tasks on time. Hatfield recommends that parents refrain from "telling" their children what they "should" do and instead provide them with tools, such as alarms on their phones or a calendar to schedule out tasks, to help them learn to plan.

5. Consider Time

Teach your adolescent the same regard for time. Some adolescents have difficulty keeping note of time, which causes them to be perpetually late. Even though wearing a watch or setting a timer on a mobile device is unlikely to address all time management issues, it can be a useful tool to always be aware of the time.

6. Help Them Master Technological Distractions

Although there are numerous technical advantages, there are academic disadvantages. In particular, these devices are very distracting. Create a list of the numerous ways that cell phones distract adolescents. Then, assist your adolescent in considering methods for reducing distractions. This will teach him to set limits while resolving problems, a skill he will need to develop in college.

Chapter 4: The Productivity Strategy That Saved My Life

Today, we are transitioning from large-scale to small-scale usefulness strategies. Minimal efficiency strategies are the tools you need to improve your daily usefulness. These techniques will help you supercharge each day. Our objective going forward will be to silence that nagging feeling that you could have accomplished more throughout the day.

(Hopefully, I'm not the only one with this issue; if not, I'll need to see the advisor on Day 2)

You currently have a list of everything you want to accomplish today from Day 3. Now, we will determine how to concentrate on this summary in order to generate the greatest return and influence our daily speculation. This skill will help you achieve your goals more quickly than those who simply set goals and establish a routine that few people can follow.

Using the ABCDE Method, even on days when you only work for a short time, you will have completed tasks that will take you further than the vast majority of items on your list combined.

Most people begin their day by completing quick and straightforward tasks. They read messages, return phone calls, and perform other low-value tasks. Not you anymore, effectively.

You are an elite performer in terms of efficacy. You only care about completing your actual work so that you can get closer to your objectives. This is what successful people concentrate on.

Every minute spent planning can save up to ten minutes during execution. This means that you can save up to two hours per day by devoting time to design. Handling your assignments in order of importance will provide you with more energy throughout the day and keep you moving forward.

The ABCDE Method is a straightforward method for organizing your day so that you prioritize completing your most important tasks first. This procedure was taught to me by self-improvement guru Brian Tracy. I do not know if he succeeded, but I will give him credit in some respects. Since I've been using it for some time, I have no idea how I ever managed without it.

In fact, I do know how: I was demonstrably less productive.

Using the ABCDE Procedure:

First, compose a list of everything you want to accomplish for the day.

Step2: Write an A next to your afternoon's most important assignment. This is the errand that will have consequences if it is not completed that day. Assuming you operate in an office, this report may need to be submitted. If you operate a business, your consumer may be required to fulfill this request.

Regardless, these are the duties you must complete that day. If you have multiple items that suit this category, simply number them A1, A2, A3, etc. Never include more than three A duties on your daily list. This will force you to focus solely on the day's most essential tasks.

The third step involves your B errands. These are the tasks that, if left undone, will have negligible but still acceptable consequences. These outcomes would be undesirable but would have no lasting effects. This could include responding to a customer complaint or paying a bill before it becomes delinquent.

Step four: C tasks are straightforward. These are the duties whose non-completion will have absolutely no consequence. This may include returning a phone call, writing a thank-you note, or organizing files.

Step 5: When in doubt about a rule of thumb, you should designate everything you can. This allows you to devote more effort to the tasks that have the greatest impact. Examine your list for anything you can provide for another person and still achieve satisfactory results. Place a D next to these endeavors. This will assist you in sifting through all of the projects on which you shouldn't spend your time in the first place.

Step 6: The E tasks are those that will be eliminated entirely. This is distinct from delegation because these duties do not need to be completed. This could include chatting with a colleague, perusing the newspaper, etc. You may have time for these, but only if you have completed everything else on your to-do list.

The ABCDE Method entails beginning your highest-priority projects first and working on them until they are completed. You never begin a B assignment if you still have an A assignment to complete.

Also, avoid jumping between duties. Develop the discipline to complete each task before moving on to the next. This will instill the habit of completing your real work first and transform you into a more useful person than you have been in recent memory.

Pop-Up Tasks

It would be absurd to assert that nothing else will be added to your schedule as the day progresses. I have regarded this as perhaps the highest test of time management. You have developed the skills necessary to deal with these interruptions.

I have developed a few principles for managing tasks that suddenly arise:

- If it's a genuine emergency, handle it immediately and then return to work.
- If it's not an emergency, ignore it for 30 minutes or until you've completed the task you were pursuing prior to being interrupted. This will prevent you from entering responsive mode and surveying the area with an erroneous sense of priority.
- After 30 minutes, take a look at the spring up task and determine where it belongs on your afternoon schedule. Is it a task A, B, C, D, or E? From then on, add it to the summary where it belongs and continue with the day's tasks.

This may appear straightforward, but it is quite possibly the most challenging task. When an extra assignment is added arbitrarily to our schedule, it can throw everything off. You had an agreement, but something has now thrown it out of balance. Your underlying intent will be to swiftly relocate it so that everything is readjusted.

That may succeed the first time, but what about the subsequent occasions? What occurs if five unexpected tasks arise within a few hours? What happens when a seemingly straightforward task consumes three hours of your time?

It may seem preposterous, but I assure you that it occurs more frequently than you realize. You will become a slave to ad hoc assignments if you don't learn how to manage them effectively. Place them where they belong; do not prioritize their needs over the work that brings you closer to your goals and greater success in life.

Chapter 5: How Developing Positive Habits

Enhancing Your Time Management

Time management is one of the most difficult skills to master. Attempting to distinguish between things that are essential in your life and those that are crucially important can be confusing and difficult. In terms of health concerns, the ability to distinguish between these factors becomes practical. The challenging aspect of health issues is that the most essential aspect of health does not typically appear imperative. For instance, going to the gym today may not be imperative, but it is unquestionably essential for your long-term health. Another example would be the fact that temporary stress won't destroy your body, but if you can't resolve the underlying issues that are causing the stress, you may find yourself in a downward spiral. Consuming processed foods, fast food, or convenient foods will increase your likelihood of becoming physically ailing, but will have no effect on your emotional state. On your path to success, it is of the utmost importance that you manage your time in order to consume healthily and take care of your body.

Dedicated to Physical Health

This may be the simplest and most difficult category to concentrate on. It is simple because all that is required is to exercise and consume well. It is difficult because few people actually create and adhere to a plan to improve their physical health. This is because we do not believe we have enough time to consume healthfully and exercise. Start your exercise regimen by devoting 20 minutes per day to physical activity. This could include anything from yoga in the morning to a 20-minute walk after dinner. The key is to enjoy exercise and incorporate it into your daily regimen. Ensure you discover a daily activity that you not only enjoy but also have the time for. Focus on a task that is simple to initiate with a quality process. As you become accustomed to setting aside time for exercise, you can gradually increase the duration and intensity of your workouts. Regular physical activity is an excellent way to reduce tension, clear your mind, and maintain your health, all of which will help you avoid burnout.

Eating a healthy diet is also extremely essential for reducing stress and preventing burnout. When you nourish your body with nutritious foods, such as fruits and vegetables, proteins, and healthy lipids, you feel better than if you consumed only processed or fast food.

When it comes to eating healthily, planning ahead and writing down your purchasing list can serve as accountability tools. Include an abundance of fruits and vegetables, proteins, and limit the amount of carbohydrates in your weekly meal planning. Planning your meals in advance can save you time and prevent you from stopping at the fast food drive-through on your way home from work.

Chapter 6: The Advantages Of Effective Time Management

Why do some individuals appear to make greater use of their time than others, when we all have the same 24 hours? The solution is effective time management.

Time management is the process of organizing and planning how to allocate time to different duties. You will end up working wiser, not harder, to accomplish more in less time, even when time is limited and demands are high.

The best performers have exceptional time management skills. And by utilizing the time-management tools provided by Mind Tools, you too can maximize your time immediately!

When you effectively manage your time, you may be able to reap numerous benefits. This includes increased output and effectiveness.

Less tension.

A higher professional standing.

Increased opportunities for advancement.

Additional opportunities to pursue your personal and professional goals.

Overall, you begin to feel more in charge, with the assurance to choose how to best utilize your time.

And by feeling happier, calmer, and more able to concentrate, you are in an excellent position to assist others in achieving their goals as well.

How effectively do you manage time?

Start by evaluating your current approach. How proficient are you at managing your time so that you can effectively complete the most important tasks? Can you effectively divide your time among various activities? And when you do find the opportunity to complete a task, are you able to focus and complete it?

Effective time management requires a shift in focus from activities to outcomes. Being occupied is not equivalent to being productive. In actuality, many individuals are less productive the busier they are.

Good Time Management Toools

Mind Tools contains a variety of resources designed to improve your time management in general. These provide actual solutions to common time management issues as well as methods for improving significant behaviors.

How to Be More Organized explains why your circumstances must be as organized as your mind! There are practical suggestions from highly organized individuals, including suggestions for leveraging technology to gain greater time management control.

And because effective time management requires planning, documenting, and remarking on your actions, we discuss some of the most well-known techniques for achieving this, such as Activity Logs, To-Do Lists, and Action Programs.

Prioritization
You may be able to accomplish more when you devote time to the appropriate activities. But how can you determine what these items are?

Scheduling
You may be aware of your obligations, but when should you carry them out? Timing is crucial.As explained in Is This a "Morning" Task?, it is advantageous to complete difficult tasks while you are still feeling alert.

And by reading How to Meet a Deadline, you can increase your efficacy, earn people's trust, and use adrenaline to your advantage.

Target Setting
The most effective "time managers" have clearly defined objectives. They establish SMART goals, which aids in time management.

Treasure Mapping is an effective method for visualizing your goals so that you are motivated to devote the time they require. Personal Mission Statements are also useful for staying organized and focused on your goals.

Concentration and Attention
Making the time to pursue your priorities is insufficient. You must also utilize this time effectively. Time Management in Implementation
Even with the best of intentions and a plethora of effective strategies, it is all too easy to fall back into poor time management habits. Consequently, Mind

Tools provides an abundance of resources to help you stay on track.

How to Stop Procrastinating, for instance, discusses why putting things off is so appealing and how to stop doing it.

Utilizing Your Free Time Wisely ensures that you do not waste a single second. And in Self-Discipline, we discuss the essential skills you'll need to implement long-term time management practices.

Time management is the process of organizing your time so that you can use it more effectively.

The benefits of effective time management include increased productivity, decreased tension, and more time to pursue what is important.

Mind Tools offers a variety of resources to improve your time management skills. They may enable you to be more organized, establish better priorities, and execute tasks with greater concentration and efficiency.

Our tools also instruct you on how to establish time management objectives, allowing you to remain motivated and disciplined.

And there is advice on overcoming common time-management issues so that you continue to refine your approach – and maximize your time usage!

Have you ever pondered why some people appear to have enough time to accomplish everything they desire, while others are continuously rushing from task to task and never complete anything? It cannot be that some individuals have less work than others. It is much more likely that they are spending their time more efficiently, or demonstrating strong time management skills.

Time management is the skill of spending one's time judiciously and effectively. You can also think of time management as the ability to complete all necessary tasks without feeling overburdened. In actuality, it is substantially more difficult than it appears. This book addresses some of the fundamentals of effective time management.

The Importance of Time Administration

We rarely, if ever, have enough time to complete everything that is expected of us or that we would like to accomplish.

Time management is defined as spending your time effectively and efficiently, but what if you are working as productively as possible but still cannot complete all of your tasks? Consider time management as a combination of working efficiently and allocating time.

In other words, those who are adept at time management are proficient at getting things done. In addition, they are better at setting priorities, determining what must be done, and discarding the rest.

They are able to do so because they comprehend the distinction between imperative and important.

Urgent responsibilities require your immediate attention, but it may or may not matter whether you give them that attention.

Failure to complete 'essential' tasks may have significant consequences for you or others.

For instance, answering the phone is an imperative task. If you don't do it, the caller will hang up and you won't know why they called, which could be crucial information. However, it could also be an automated voice informing you that you may be eligible for compensation for being mis-sold insurance. That is not significant.

According to conventional wisdom, regular dental care is crucial. If you do not, you could develop periodontal disease or other complications. But it's not essential. However, if you wait too long, it may become essential because you may develop toothache.

The act of picking up your children from school is essential and vital. If you are late, children will be anxiously waiting on the playground or in the classroom, wondering where you are. You may also inconvenience others, such as instructors who are awaiting your arrival with your children.

Reading amusing emails and browsing Facebook are neither imperative nor essential. Why then is it the very first action you do each day?

This distinction between imperative and important is the key to allocating your time and tasks, whether you're at work, at home, or in school.

It helps you determine which tasks should be completed first and which can be deferred or skipped altogether. For instance, if you put off imperative but unimportant work, you may find that it becomes unnecessary.

Using a grid similar to the preceding priority matrix could help you categorize your responsibilities.

The Priority Matrix allows you to categorize tasks based on their urgency and importance.

Utilization of the Priority Matrix
To effectively utilize the priority matrix, it is necessary to evaluate your tasks daily. daily: question yourself:

Which of my tasks must be finished within the next 48 hours?

These are the 'Urgent' tasks.

Which of the imperative responsibilities are the most essential?

It is advisable to enumerate your responsibilities in order of importance, rather than classifying them as either "important" or "not important."

Which of the non-urgent tasks are the most essential?

Again, it is preferable to arrange them in order rather than give them absolute distinctions.

Now, using the answers to these questions and the following principles, allocate your tasks to the boxes of the priority matrix:

Each package should contain approximately seven or eight assignments maximum.

Start by checking the 'Do Now' box.

Importantly, do not put off important or crucial tasks because they are disagreeable. They will not improve by postponing.

If you must consume a frog, you should do so first thing in the morning. And if you must consume two amphibians, it is best to consume the largest one first.

Next, consider the less pressing but still important tasks. Plan time in your schedule to complete them, or contemplate outsourcing them to someone else, after deciding what you will do with them.

Delegate the essential but less important tasks.

Now eliminate the non-critical and non-urgent duties.

Complete the assignment. Create a "To Do" agenda. After completing it, move on to the next assignment or duties.

If you have more work than you can manage in any quadrant, you should a) do some, b) delegate some, and c) eliminate some.

Regular pruning of your matrix in this manner will ensure that you can focus on what is essential and maintain a steady flow of work.

An individual judgment

The significance and/or urgency of work is not immutable. You alone can determine what you perceive to be significant or essential.

Some individuals, for instance, prefer to wait until they are asked for a task a second time before beginning to complete it. If they are never asked again, they will never begin the work because they will conclude that it is not a priority for anyone.

Also, remember that you and your health are essential. Even if you have a lengthy to-do list, it is still important to get some exercise, take a 10-minute walk, and find time to consume well. You should prioritize your physical and mental health over 'essential' activities.

Importance and/or urgency are not immutable conditions. You should frequently evaluate your to-do list to ensure that nothing should be prioritized because it has become more imperative and/or important.

What can be done if an essential task is repeatedly pushed to the bottom of the to-do list in favor of more imperative but still essential tasks?

First, determine its importance. Does it actually need to be done, or have you simply been convincing yourself that it does?

Individual versus Professional

How do you reconcile your personal and professional responsibilities? There are two ways to handle this situation:

Advantages: your belongings are not misplaced.

You will need to establish a balance between business and personal belongings.

Use two separate matrices, and allot distinct processing times for each.

Advantages: demonstrates that you can handle both with a realistic view of urgency.

Negatives: may become increasingly problematic.

It is ultimately your decision; the important thing is to make it work for you.

Additional Principles of Effective Time Management

Therefore, the priority matrix is essential for prioritizing your mission. However, time management is about more than just setting priorities; it also involves working more efficiently. There are a variety of ways in which you can increase your efficiency and output.

Keep Tidy

For some of us, debris can be a genuine distraction and a source of distress.

Organizing may boost both self-esteem and motivation. Additionally, you will find it easier to stay on top of things if your workstation is organized and you keep your systems up to date.

Best Tip for Cleaning:
Create three piles for your belongings: Keep, Donate, and Discard.
Maintain it if you need to retain it for your records, or use it for whatever purpose you see fit. Add anything that necessitates action to your task list.
If you don't want something, but someone else could use it, or if it is labor that can and should be assigned, give it away.
Throw away (or recycle) items that you or others have no use for.

Use A 'To Do List
Lists, whether electronic or on paper, are an excellent way to remember what you have to do and to see at a glance what you have neglected.

Consider emphasizing the most important duties in some way, and remove items from your list when they are complete or no longer necessary.

Choose Your Moment

Everyone has times of the day when they are most productive. It is prudent to schedule the most difficult tasks for these times. However, you must also schedule activities that must be completed at specific times, such as meetings and trips to the post office.

Prepare a list of important but non-urgent tasks that can be completed in the ten minutes between meetings. For example, this may be the ideal time to send that email confirming your vacation dates.

Using Scheduling Technology

Some people still prefer to use a paper calendar and to-do list, which is fine.

However, for those who value technology, there are currently a variety of scheduling tools available. Apps such as Doodle, Calendly, Microsoft Bookings, and Google Calendar can help you plan your work and schedule meetings with others.

You may also provide predetermined appointment windows for people to schedule meetings with you, while concealing the remainder of your schedule. This means that you can schedule 'me-time' or family time without fretting about what others will think or whether they will attempt to override your priorities.

This allows you to automate your meetings without relinquishing control of your time to a third party.

Don't Put Things Off, But Do Ask WhysYou's Tempted

If a task is important and essential, get to work.

However, if you find yourself making excuses for not taking action, consider why.

You may be uncertain as to whether you should undertake the assignment. Perhaps you have ethical concerns, or you do not believe it to be the best alternative. If so, you may find that others concur. Discuss it with coworkers or your boss if you're at work, and family or friends if you're at home, and see if there is a superior option.

Try Not to Multitask

Since it takes time for our minds to refocus, most people are not adept at multitasking.

It is preferable to finish one task before beginning another. If you have a number of tasks to complete, try to group them together and complete related tasks sequentially.

Remain Calm and Maintain Perspective

Perhaps the most important thing to remember is to maintain your composure. Feeling overburdened by too many responsibilities can be extremely distressing. Remember that the world will likely not end if you do not complete your final task of the day or if you postpone it until the next day, especially if you have set your priorities correctly.

Going home or getting an early night so that you are rested for the following day may be a superior alternative to meeting a self-imposed or external deadline that may not even be significant.

Take a moment to pause and put your life and priorities in perspective, and you may find that your perspective has changed substantially!

Chapter 7: Why Effective Time Management Is Crucial

Numerous successful individuals have arrived at their current position via various routes. But they all have one thing in common: they know how to reconcile ambitious endeavors with those that will help them advance.

"Why should I spend extra time planning how to spend my time if I'm already running through the day?"

I am glad you asked.

If you're like me, you dislike the tension of running out of time on anything. I will demonstrate how to manage your time and clarify why it is crucial to do so in order to achieve personal success. You are aware of the distinction between working hard and working intelligently, and you prefer the latter. There is always more to do, even when time is limited. This is the secret of successful people.

People who cannot manage their time produce low-quality work and are constantly anxious because they are under constant pressure. It is difficult to think of someone you know who has a lot of work and a lot of other things going on simultaneously. Because this person is always in a hurry, you can infer that the quality of their work is poor, even though they appear to be very busy.

When there are multiple tasks contending for our attention at the same time, we resort to inefficient multitasking to complete everything. How then do some individuals accomplish so much more in a day than others? Given the abundance of applications, methods, and ideas available from a variety of sources, you might believe that time management entails recording your tasks in calendars and planners in order to keep track of them.

If you do not comprehend why time management is so important, you will lack the motivation to make the necessary adjustments. Here are a few reasons why effective time management is crucial and advantageous.

Time management increases productivity and efficiency.

You should consider how much labor you can complete before the deadline. Imagine how much better your job would be if you weren't forced to take shortcuts due to being late. As long as you plan your time well, you won't be in a hurry, but you will still want to make progress. Having a strong desire and a great deal of freedom to work at your own tempo will aid you in producing excellent results.

You gained a sense of accomplishment.

As soon as your time management efforts begin to bear fruit in the form of accomplishments, your job satisfaction will increase. If you learn how to effectively manage your time, you will be able to live a happier life because you will be able to seize more opportunities that you may have overlooked in the past.

What if you must simultaneously be at work and at home? In that case, you will be unable to engage in genuinely satisfying activities outside of work, such as volunteering or assisting those in need. These activities are beneficial to your psyche and can enhance your life. It is worthwhile to devote your time to something you find enjoyable and consider essential.

You are Free of Stress

Your level of tension is directly proportional to your time management skills. You will have fewer unpleasant surprises and more time to unwind as a result. You will not rush from one task to another. People who are constantly occupied but never complete anything or their work are stressed. By providing you with greater control over your time, time management skills can help alleviate some of your tension. Your ability to meet deadlines will improve over time, allowing you to remain calm while working. Having a solid understanding of how to spend your time provides peace of mind.

It helps you develop greater self-discipline.

Good time management implies that you are highly self-disciplined and adhere to your deadlines and objectives. In all aspects of your existence, self-discipline is beneficial. It is beneficial to your health, relationships, and career. To increase the likelihood of achieving your objectives in any aspect of your life, improve your time management skills. This will increase your self-control, which will increase your likelihood of achieving your objectives.

Enhances your ability to make sound choices

Effective time management skills will allow you to avoid tension and set aside sufficient time each night to sleep adequately. People who don't get enough sleep make poor judgments that affect nearly every aspect of their personal and professional lives. When you have excellent time management skills, you can avoid making poor decisions because you won't be fatigued or anxious.

To be more organized and avoid making errors, give yourself sufficient time to consider your next steps. You create more labor for yourself if you disregard minor details or do things incorrectly. You can eliminate the need to repeat a task if you are able to make appropriate choices from the outset.

Now that you are aware of the benefits of effective time management, let's examine what you can do to begin developing this crucial skill.

Chapter 8: Time Management: What Is It?

It is correct to say, "Time and tide wait for no one." To be successful in all aspects of life, an individual must understand the value of time. Those who are sedentary are those who fail to develop their own personality. Time management refers to effectively monitoring time so that the right opportunity is allocated to the right action.

Time management is the most prevalent method of planning and organizing how to divide one's time between various activities. You will maintain a flexible perspective if you hit the mark, allowing you to accomplish more than expected in less time - regardless of time constraints and pressures. Time management is the most prevalent method for planning and controlling the duration of straightforward activities. Excellent time management enables a person to accomplish more in a shorter amount of time, reduces stress, and promotes professional success.

Effective time management enables individuals to assign specific time slots to activities based on their importance. Time management refers to utilizing time because time is always limited. Consider which action is more important and how much time should be allocated to identical tasks. Determine which tasks should be completed first and which can be completed later. Time management is crucial in both our personal and professional lives.

Utilizing time management includes:

Effective Preparation
Developing aims and objectives
Setting deadlines
The assignment of responsibilities
Putting activities in order of importance
Spending the proper amount of time on the proper activity

1. Strategic Planning.
Plan your day well in advance. Create a daily schedule or "undertaking plan". Record the essential tasks that must be completed in a single day alongside the amount of time that must be allocated to each task. High Need work should be prioritized, followed by tasks that do not require as much of your attention right now. Complete upcoming responsibilities independently. Try not to begin new responsibilities until you have concluded your previous obligations. Check the items that you

have proactively completed. Ensure you complete the tasks within the allotted time frame.

Setting Goals And Objectives.
Working without objectives and focus in an organization would be analogous to the captain of a ship becoming lost at sea. You would indeed be stranded. Set objectives for yourself and ensure that they are practical and attainable.

3. Setting Deadlines.
Set deadlines for yourself and work diligently to complete responsibilities before the deadlines. Try not to assume that your supervisor will always ask you something. Determine how to assume responsibility for. You are the finest person to set the cutoff times. Consider how much time should be devoted to a specific task and for how long. Utilize a planner to compare the important dates to the specified termination times.

4. Delegation Of Responsibilities.

Determine how to state "NO" in the workplace. Try to avoid doing everything by yourself. There are also others. One should not acknowledge that something is difficult for him. In order for representatives to meet deadlines, tasks and responsibilities should be assigned in accordance with their intrigue and area of expertise. A person who does not understand something requires more time than a person who has mastered the task.

Prioritizing activities based on their significance.
Concentrate on the tasks according to their significance and importance. Understand the distinction between significant and urgent duties. Recognize which tasks must be completed within at least a day, which must be completed

within at least a month, etc. The most important tasks should be completed first.

Time Management Implications.

How about we also consider the consequences of inadequate time management?

Poor work procedure.
Lack of preparation and adherence to objectives indicates a lack of proficiency. For instance, if there are a number of significant tasks to complete, a persuasive plan involves completing related tasks concurrently or sequentially. However, if you don't plan, you may end up zigzagging or moving backwards as you carry out your responsibilities. This results in decreased efficacy and output.

The loss of leisure.
Poor time management results in time squandered. By conversing with friends via web-based entertainment while performing a task, for instance, you are distracting yourself and have nothing to do.

3. Loss of control.
You experience a loss of control over your life as a result of your lack of comprehension regarding the upcoming endeavor. This can contribute to increased anxiety and apprehension.

The work is of poor quality.
Usually, poor time management causes the quality of your work to suffer. As an example, rushing to complete responsibilities with no time to spare typically compromises quality.
5. Poor posture.

If clients and your manager cannot rely on you to complete tasks as soon as possible, their expectations and perception of you are negatively affected. If a client cannot rely on you to complete a task on time, they will likely move their business elsewhere.

Chapter 9: The Day As It Actually Occurs

You rest twice through the rest caution. (You're exhausted from yesterday's grappling match and today's schedule.) No time for practice or breakfast, which was not included in the initial summary. You're down two and feeling regretful and irritable before you've even begun.

You examine your gathering notes, scan the left-hand section of the Journal's first page, and dash to the vehicle. You are blessed with good luck. The vehicle starts despite the fact that you've neglected to have it serviced - there's no time. No idiot will spoil your day by passing you, and traffic flows reasonably well.

Even so, the journey requires 18.5 minutes, so you are currently 90 seconds behind schedule. Likewise, you were unable to listen to your persuasive CD because the vehicle's CD player was broken. (You should add "sort CD player out" to your list of prospective tasks.)

You can anticipate the remainder. (You need not anticipate it. You've been there.) You don't even come close to reading the entire phone message, let alone the email. The gathering typically begins late and lasts a long time, correct? It is too late to complete the quarterly report, so you spend the remainder of the morning on the phone and responding to e-mails.

After a lunch you didn't eat and a meeting you didn't need, you finally have a few minutes to complete those quarterly report notes. You're exhausted, irritable, stuffed with a chicken enchilada that won't settle down and allow itself to be processed, and preoccupied with the urgent gathering you must attend. Unsurprisingly, the report will not coordinate itself.

Another gathering (begins late, lasts long), another stomach-churning drive, and a wasted stop at the dry cleaners (you left your case ticket on the bureau in your haste earlier today).

Another daytime photograph.

And now is the time to commence the next shift, the business day shift at home sweet home.

Quite a horrifying spectacle, no? Also, this is not precisely an exaggeration.

Did the daily schedule assist? Sure. It provided a record of what you didn't complete while you were working on other tasks, and it aided you in going to bed culpable and confused for each unfinished task.

What did not go well? You failed to anticipate the unexpected. You lacked practicality regarding your own abilities and the required persistence to complete tasks. You neglected important items that should have been completed and spent a great deal of time on low-priority tasks.

Simply stated, this was not a daily occurrence. It was a list of items to obtain, a dream, an unattainable dream, a request for disappointment and exhaustion.

Chapter 10: Beginning With Module One

Typically, time management training begins with objective setting. These objectives are documented and may be decomposed into a project, an action plan, or a plain task list. Then, activities are rated based on urgency and importance, designated priorities, and deadlines are set. This procedure yields a plan containing a task list or schedule of activities. Routine and repetitive tasks are frequently given less priority than tasks that contribute to essential goals.

A skill set consisting of personal motivation, delegation skills, organization tools, and crisis management should support the entire process. In this workshop, we will discuss all of the above and more.

Atelier Objectives

Consistently, research has demonstrated that when explicit objectives are associated with learning, it is easier and more rapid. Keeping this in mind, let's review our daily objectives.

At the conclusion of this workshop, participants should be able to: • Plan and prioritize each day's activities in a more efficient, productive manner • Overcome procrastination quickly and easily • Handle crises effectively and quickly • Organize your workspace and workflow to make better use of time • Delegate more effectively • Use rituals to make your life run more smoothly

Encourage participants to record their own workshop objectives in their respective guides.

Pre-Assignment Evaluation

The objective of the Pre-Assignment is to prompt participants to consider the time management strategies they currently employ and the areas in which they can improve.

We asked respondents:

- What are your most significant time-wasters?
- What are you doing to regulate your time currently?
- What could you improve upon?
- If you only took away one thing from this workshop, what would it be?

Discuss these questions and record your responses on the flip chart. Attempt to reach a group consensus on every item.

Decluttering your schedule requires deliberate effort. As the Annie Dillard quote states, "how we spend our days is, of course, how we spend our lives." This is not always a simple task.

Whether you use a pen and paper planner, an app on your phone to manage your calendar, or another method to keep your day organized, spend some time analyzing how you've spent the past few weeks and what you have planned for the upcoming weeks.

How many of these tasks excite you? These are the ones you'll want to prioritize; they are the things that invigorate you. These can be kept.

And how many of them tire you out or cause you anxiety?

We won't unilaterally cancel all of these obligations, but we will evaluate them to determine if we need to keep them all.

There are multiple tasks you must complete. Things like your annual physical, your dog's veterinary appointment, and your child's graduation. Some of these products are immovable and cannot be delayed.

However, certain activities can be rearranged if you need a bit more breathing room or have set yourself up for a difficult day by squeezing them between other obligations or engagements.

There may also be items that you aren't enthusiastic about and have no idea why they're there in the first place. Optional work-related activities, social engagements, and others may appear essential when you accept an invitation or schedule them on your calendar, but you are not required to participate.

These are the items you can eliminate entirely from your calendar. And although you may feel a little terrible as you send those cancellation messages or erase those appointments from your calendar, by the end of the day you will feel as though a burden has been lifted from your shoulders.

Many of us wake up with jam-packed schedules because we simply cannot decline engagements.

Coffe with a colleague? Sure! Your friend's child's birthday party? Why then? Do you shop with a friend? I can achieve that...

Although you may feel bad about declining invitations to chill out, get together, and have fun, protecting your time and peace of mind is crucial.

To free your schedule, you must learn to say no and do so consistently. If you are unsure about committing to something, give yourself time and space to consider the request before responding. This will require discipline if you have a tendency to say "yes."

Mastering the phrase "Thank you, I'd love to, but I can't. Maybe next time!" is a vital skill that we should all become accustomed to employing whenever plans arise that may interfere with your much-needed relaxation.

Creating clear schedule boundaries makes it simpler to say no. If family meals are non-negotiable, it becomes easier to say no to items that try to contend with them.

If you still find it difficult to find enough time for yourself after declining activities and decluttering your schedule, you may want to schedule specific times for yourself.

If you feel terrible saying "no" when someone requests you to join them for lunch or do them a favor, here is an excellent strategy to help you overcome that.

By tangibly blocking the time on your calendar, you are consciously making room for yourself to relax, breathe, and take care of whatever you need – which is just as important as all the other demands that are being placed on you by others.

Self-care should be on your list of priorities. When you set aside time for self-care, you'll be better suited to handle all of your essential responsibilities.

Chapter 11: The Workings Of Time Management

Developing a habit of doing the right thing at the right time will enable you to devote the appropriate amount of time to the right activity.Incorrectly completed work serves little purpose.Avoid devoting an entire day to activities that can be completed in less than an hour.In addition, schedule time for personal phone calls and Facebook and Twitter updates.In the end, humans are not devices.

To effectively manage your time, you must: • Organize: Do not litter your desk with file containers and stacks of paper.Don't keep anything you don't need.Arrange essential documents in folders.Label each file and place it in the appropriate filing cabinet compartment. It saves time spent on unproductive searches.

• Do not squander time loitering or conversing about others. Concentrate on your tasks and complete them on time. Remember that your employer does not pay you to observe other employees' cubicles or to play computer games. First, complete your tasks, and then do as you please. Do not delay until the last minute.

• Focus: Effective time management requires concentration.

• Develop the habit of using planners, organizers, and tabletop calendars to enhance your time management. Use your mobile devices or personal computers to set alarms.

History of time administration

People have always searched for better and faster ways to complete tasks, whether it was a more efficient way to catch animals for food or a friction-based method for starting a fire. Prior to the latter half of the 1800s and the beginning of the 1900s, however, no one adopted a deliberate, scientific approach to completing tasks more quickly and with less effort. Frederick Winslow Taylor is typically regarded as the originator of scientific management. In 1911, he published The Principles of Scientific Management, which, along with the work of Frank and Lillian Gilbreth, laid the groundwork for the modern management discipline.

Chapter 12: The Adverse Effects Of Procrastination

Only when procrastination becomes endemic and begins to have a significant impact on a person's daily life does it become a more serious issue for that person. It is not simply a matter of having poor time management skills in these situations; it is a significant aspect of their way of living.

Perhaps they are delinquent in paying their bills, procrastinating the start of major projects until the night before the deadline, waiting until the day before a birthday to go shopping for gifts, and even submitting their tax returns.

Unfortunately, procrastination can have a significant impact on a person's mental health, as well as their social, professional, and financial wellbeing:

An increase in both stress and disease prevalence
There is an increased emphasis on interpersonal connections.
One's family, acquaintances, coworkers, and fellow students' resentment
The consequences of not timely paying one's bills or submitting one's taxes

How to conquer procrastination

At some point, you may find yourself inquiring, "How can I stop procrastinating?"

You are in luck, as there are a variety of strategies you can employ to combat procrastination and complete tasks promptly. You might consider them your procrastination exercises.

You can learn as much as you want about self-discipline, motivation, planning, and time management, but if you don't incorporate what you've learned into your daily routine, habits, thinking patterns, and mental models, the information will be useless and merely stored in your memory.

The query now is, what tools can you utilize to stop procrastinating?

Personal vision: One of the most important tools is the personal vision, which not only helps you understand your capabilities and priorities, but also ensures that you will never again ponder what you wish to accomplish with the rest of your life. In addition, the personal vision may aid you in focusing your efforts on the most essential tasks and organizing your priorities so that you are not continuously switching between tasks. If you can identify what motivates you, you will be able to maintain your discipline and maximize each day.

The accumulation of duties on lengthy to-do lists is a common contributor to procrastination. When we view the extensive list of tasks that need to be completed, we may become so enraged that we give up on completing them. In addition to assisting you in prioritizing the work that is already on your calendar and reducing the number of new responsibilities, the To-Do Today method is designed to facilitate the daily completion of the most important and time-sensitive tasks. You will be able to accomplish significantly more in a day while experiencing significantly less anxiety and fatigue.

Developing new behaviors is one of the primary pillars of personal development. As something becomes a habit, it requires less mental effort to continue doing it on a regular basis. Consequently, establishing new habits should be a high priority. Nonetheless, there are numerous misunderstandings regarding what is effective and what is not in the process of acquiring new habits. The Habit list was developed using findings from scientific studies on effective planning, the acquisition of habits, and the monitoring of these aspects, which further motivates us.

Having a Conversation with Myself: This instrument will assist in guiding you through your very own "Meeting With Yourself," a time period set aside just for you! Throughout your sessions, you may choose to focus on long-term planning and an overall assessment of your personal development. It is intended to encourage self-reflection by prompting you to consider how far you have come in recent years. Consider the direction you would like your life to take and the aspects of yourself that may need further development.

Chapter 13: Replace The Slave Insect

You must be certain that you differentiate between taking a brief break to refresh your mind and procrastination. You shouldn't expect your home-based business to break records if your favorite days are the ones you spend away from it, and if the only thing that motivates you is spending hours viewing "boob tube." If you lack motivation at work, you may wish to select a business model that is more aligned with your interests.

However, if you recall how much you appreciate creating websites, online marketing, and other aspects of working from home, it is unlikely that work is the problem. You've probably acquired the laziness bug.

If your work still inspires you, particularly when you see the results of your efforts, you will create a more ambitious plan to do more. Instead of allowing the grass grow under your feet, you should begin working on your home business.

USE TIME INTELLIGENTLY

It is simple to become so busy operating a home-based business that the task of time management becomes overwhelming. If you don't effectively manage your time, the flexible schedule you've come to appreciate can lead to procrastination and laziness.

The first stage in time management is to create a schedule of all regularly scheduled meetings and appointments. This will allow you to specify available time on your calendar. If you do not already have a day planner or other time management instrument, you should purchase one immediately. A rudimentary day planner can be purchased at a local store for a few dollars.

Schedule some time for relaxation. If you have extra time after scheduling all of your responsibilities, examine it to determine where it can be reduced. You may have scheduled an hour to pick up your daughter from daycare, but you can do so in thirty minutes, leaving you with a half-hour buffer.

Ensure that everyone in your family combines their individual schedules in order to schedule family activities. Even though it is easy to become overburdened when running your own business, it is essential that you schedule time with your family and do not allow anything to prevent you from attending important appointments. Keep your day planner with you at all times so that you can record new appointments as they are made. Making last-minute plans could land you in serious difficulty. Keeping your day planner near will help you stay on track and allow you to prepare for any unforeseen events.

LAXITY OR FEAR

If you want to find a remedy for lethargy, you must first determine its root cause. You must determine the source of your lethargy. As with anything else, it is impossible to discover a solution until the problem has been precisely defined. Although we frequently presume that lazy people simply need to get their act together, there are instances in which a more fundamental issue exists.

Frequent causes of laziness are anxiety and uncertainty. The number of individuals you have encountered who continually complain about their jobs but do nothing to improve them. This is the consequence of their dread. They are terrified of failing, being negatively assessed by others, being rejected, and appearing inferior, among other things.

Actually, neither procrastination nor sloth make anyone joyful. Whether it's closing a large sale, opening a new branch, or launching a new website for your home business, we've all experienced the incredible sense of success. Willpower alone cannot cure the effects of the sluggish bug's wound. The only way to stop being lethargic is to identify your anxieties and acquire the skills necessary to overcome them. Occasionally, specialist assistance may be required.

CONQUERING LAZINESS

Laziness, delay, and commerce do not go together well. You want individuals to associate your brand with fervor, inspiration, motivation, and perseverance. The following tips may assist you in overcoming your propensity for inaction and getting your home-based business back on track:

You must first determine what is holding you back and preventing you from achieving your objectives. Frequently, the issue is not as significant as you believe, and resolving it is simple. Regardless of the difficulty, you must discover a way to overcome it.

Determine if your problem is something you can neglect, get assistance with, or abandon. Frequently, the business proprietor is simply an excessive perfectionist.

Determine to get started on the necessary task and to see it through to completion.

Break down large tasks into a series of smaller tasks and concentrate on completing one tiny element at a time.

Tell yourself that you want to complete the task immediately. Sometimes it is even useful to say it out loud.

After completing each minor task, take a moment to congratulate yourself and encourage yourself to continue.

Establish long-term objectives that will provide you with something to look forward to and serve as motivation to continue.

Use common sense to keep the sluggish insect out of your ear. If you are aware that labor must be completed, do it. Do not wait until the last minute.Even if you operate a business from home, you should set an alarm and get out of bed as if you were going to work. Dress yourself, take a shower, and put on your shoes. If you spend the entire day in pajamas, it is easier to be indolent. If you must pass by your bed later in the day, do so as soon as you emerge from it. Otherwise, it will not appear quite as inviting. There are multiple ways to combat laziness; choose one that works and stay with it.

Chapter 14: Commence The Day Properly

Instead of moving out of bed, it is simple to use your smartphone to press the snooze button or remain in bed. However, these actions waste time. Once you have established a routine, it is simpler to avoid bad habits and form healthy ones. Before coming to work, you may begin eating a healthy breakfast, practicing mindfulness, or even engaging in daily exercise. You will maintain healthy habits for the remainder of your existence. You might begin consuming healthier, exercising more frequently, and using your phone less.

Improving Your Relationships

A morning routine can have an effect on your relationships. Stress reduction is most essential. Even if the individual has nothing to do with your problems, it is typical to release your emotions on a loved one. Because you are less agitated, you are less likely to lose your temper with others. Additionally, a morning routine can make you more approachable to your family, which is essential for fostering stronger bonds. You will have additional time to spend with your family if you are more organized.

It is impossible to exaggerate the importance of developing a daily schedule for enhancing relationships with household members. When your family members or roommates are aware of your morning ritual, they can plan accordingly. Since there will be no contention over who must use the restroom, there will also be no problems if two or more people attempt to use the kitchen simultaneously.

Accomplish Your Objectives

Do you desire to accomplish your life's goals? Then maintaining a consistent daily schedule is the quickest route to success! You begin to exert control and construct, and the disparity becomes so pronounced over time that you accomplish significantly more than the majority of people. You now have more time and creativity, which enables you to accomplish objectives you never thought possible.

2.2 How to Establish the Ideal Morning Routine?

Your daily habits can determine the difference between a decent day and a great one. Developing healthy habits is crucial to a productive day because your productivity begins the instant you wake up.

The actions you prioritize, such as consuming a healthy breakfast, exercising, and reading, have the ability to alter your mindset. Choose a schedule that makes you joyful, prepares you to perform essential tasks, promotes flow, and enables you to maintain a healthy level of job satisfaction.

Provide Yourself Some Time

Avoid falling unconscious! In the beginning, it is challenging not to revert to old habits and press the snooze button to stay in bed a little longer. A decent daily schedule allows you sufficient time to appreciate and benefit from it.

The duration varies from person to person, but is typically between 30 and 90 minutes. It is commonly believed that in order to have a respectable morning regimen, one must now rise at 4:00 a.m. Experts in productivity recommend that you focus on yourself and assess what you can realistically accomplish and maintain. Do not worry about the accomplishments of others.

Get Your Body Moving
It is possible that your previous morning routine consisted of waking up and promptly reaching for your phone, lying

in bed for thirty minutes, reading Facebook, or even checking your work emails. Instead of focusing solely on what we can "add" to our morning routine, efficiency instructors recommend that we examine the activities we can "stop doing" when planning our morning routine.

Giving ourselves space away from the television enables us to stand, unwind, practice yoga, or take a short walk. Any morning activity is preferable to reclining in bed and browsing social media platforms! We are consciously awakening both our bodies and our minds.

If we skip this step, we run the risk of feeling hurried and ineffective throughout the day, which defeats the purpose of a healthy morning routine!

Exercise Being Stillness.

Morning meditation is equally as important as physical activity. According to Michael Hyatt, the greatest author, industrialist, and personal coach and former CEO of Thomas Nelson Publications, stillness can help us begin the day on the right foot.

Meditation, relaxation, and prayer are all excellent ways to incorporate this into your morning routine. The practice of serenity can help us feel more grounded, focused, and prepared to successfully prioritize duties. By omitting this step, we run the risk of feeling hurried and ineffective throughout the day, which defeats the purpose of a healthy morning routine!

The practice of stillness allows us to revitalize and be present in the present moment. When checking email, browsing through social media, or multitasking, we are not in the moment, which increases tension and anxiety. Practicing stillness or deep breathing exercises can help you feel calm, in control, and at ease throughout the day.

Correctly Fuel

As children, we likely heard that a good day begins with a nutritious breakfast. True, what we consume in the morning has a substantial impact on our physical health, activity levels, and mental attitude throughout the day.

When we consume foods devoid of nutritional value, we are not at our best, our activity levels fluctuate throughout the day, and we appear out of control. A nutritious meal enables us to nourish our bodies effectively, resulting in sustained energy levels and enhanced alertness and concentration.

Consider Your Day

After completing your morning regimen, it is advisable to take a moment to reflect on the upcoming day. By evaluating your day with intent, you can maintain control over your schedule instead of allowing it to dominate you.

Attempt to be truthful about the importance of specific tasks and the fact that not all of them can be a top priority. Emotionally, it may feel the same, but we cannot function in such a manner without becoming overwrought.

It is often preferable to focus on one thing at a time. Determine where your focus and efforts should be focused, then complete that task before moving on to the next. Attempting to balance multiple responsibilities may lead to ineffective time management, diminished performance, and exhaustion.

Give Yourself Sufficient Time

Whether you work at home or in an office, it is essential to give yourself enough time to physically and mentally prepare for work, particularly if you are not a morning person.

To achieve this, choose your wake-up time with consideration. In addition to obtaining eight hours of sleep, you should set alarms so that you have sufficient time to complete your morning ritual and form beneficial new habits. Regardless of the time you choose to wake up, attempt to schedule sufficient time for self-care to avoid overworking yourself.

Hydration is essential for your comfort and good health. Water consumption is a vital component of a healthy daily routine because when you feel good, you are more productive and motivated.

Consume a full glass of water upon awakening to maintain hydration. To prevent missing it, complete it before your morning cup of tea or coffee. Additionally, this prevents the fatigue induced by caffeinated beverages.

Take Deep Breaths
Relaxation can be achieved through meditation in conjunction with positive thoughts. Take time to sit with your thoughts and breathe thoroughly if you wish to develop a calming routine.
Combine your mantras with a breathing exercise technique, such as roll breathing, to establish an effective routine. To manage tension, repeat your affirmation when you are calm or want to become more relaxed.

Address Emotional and Spiritual Basics.
This is surprising because we commonly believe that high achievers rise up and run, but this is not the case for most of them. Instead, they begin their day with gratitude, introspection, prayer, if possible, time spent outdoors, meditation, and other self-care practices.

Shower with Cold Water.
There is a reason why numerous health experts recommend taking a frigid bath first thing in the morning. The frigid water improves the body's circulation, allowing more oxygen to circulate throughout the entire body. Consequently, your body is better able to combat the fatigue you experience upon waking. It has also been demonstrated that cold baths aid in weight loss and strengthen the immune system.

It is essential to remember not to immediately enter the shower when the water is chilly. Start with a hot shower and progressively lower the temperature to around 70 degrees Fahrenheit or lower, based on your preferences.

Consume A Nutrient-Dense Beverage.
There is a reason why physicians call breakfast "the most important meal of the day." Consuming nutritious foods and beverages first thing in the morning provides our bodies with vital energy, vitamins, and minerals that enable us to remain tranquil and more focused throughout the day.

While healthful eating is essential, many individuals find it challenging, particularly in the morning. If preparing and ingesting a daily meal is too time-consuming or costly, consider wellness drinks that include ginger, citrus, cayenne pepper, and essential vitamins such as Vitamins C and D. These ingredients strengthen our immune system and provide us with the nourishment we require to be productive and motivated throughout the day.

Chapter 15: Ineffective Is A Long To-Do List

If there is one thing I have learned, it is that "a long to-do list doesn't work" – you believe that the longer the items, the more productive you feel, which is not true. Long lists are nothing but guilt traps; the longer the unfinished items, the more despondent and miserable you feel.

To-do lists may be beneficial for you, but if you don't use them effectively, they may cause you to feel even more anxious, depressed, and guilty than you already do.

Advantages of a Strategic To-Do List • You are aware of what needs to be done. • You will feel less anxious because you have written down and removed from your mind all of your "to-do" items.

- It helps you organize your priorities.

- You experience a greater sense of organization; • It facilitates your planning; • You don't forget or overlook as many items.

Long Task Lists Have a Negative Impact

When you consider all the tasks you must complete, you feel so burdened.

You are uncertain of how to order the items on the list, and seeing home and work activities mixed together is confusing.

REGULATIONS FOR CREATING A TO-DO LIST

Categorize

One lie we convince ourselves is that I HAVE SO MUCH TO DO, which causes us to cram so many activities into one day. Asking yourself, "WHAT ONE ACTIVITY OR AT MOST THREE ACTIVITIES, WHEN

I DO AND ACCOMPLISH THEM, WILL MAKE MY DAY FULFILLING?" is one way to determine that we have fewer activities to complete. Once you can answer these questions, you will have identified your most important task for the day.

To determine how to prioritize your three activities into THE MOST IMPORTANT ONE TO BE COMPLETED FIRST. Classify them as Important and imperative

Not urgent but crucial

Not essential but urgent

Not vital not urgent

The first two categories are required for a productive day. Not a compendium of guilt-inducing behaviors.

We wasted our time as students and as people by focusing on the last two categories. And we claim that we lack sufficient leisure. When in fact we have sufficient leisure. We spend countless hours playing video games, chatting on social media, and conversing with friends about non-productive matters, checking our email nearly every hour, and viewing porn while claiming to be time-crunched. In actuality, these are TIME KILLERS for young people.

Your estimate is incorrect

We are poor at estimating the duration of our project. Typically, we estimate how long an undertaking will last when we have limited information. In actuality, we have no idea how long it will last. We presume that all things are equal (all things being equal). In actuality, this is not always the case.

How many times have you estimated an assignment to take 3 hours but it ended up taking the entire day? or when you intended to spend two hours at a friend's apartment but ended up spending the entire day there? Or it can happen vice versa. Humans are notoriously poor at estimation, so there is nothing wrong with you. We assume that all things are equal when, in actuality, they are not.

What you ought to do: Reduce and perform your

Prioritize important and urgent duties before you

perform other duties. Divide the duties into subtasks

modest chunks and complete them. Consequently even

If you devote the entire day to that task, you spent it on your most essential responsibilities; will make your day satisfying. Then, proceed to the subsequent endeavor.

Review

Review your daily objectives and initiatives constantly and ask, AM I ON THE RIGHT TRACK? This will assist you in organizing your existence effectively. Always ask yourself at the conclusion of each week, "Was my week fulfilling?" If yes, how can I improve it, and if no, what went wrong, find out what went wrong, and never do it again.

Enhance your planning by:

Set specific goals to improve your planning, such as "go to the library every day after my last class and spend at least two hours studying," rather than a general goal such as "study for my upcoming exam."

Break up your endeavors into manageable chunks. For instance, if you need to write an essay, you can begin by selecting a title, developing a general outline, and locating five academic references that are pertinent to your topic. It is essential to remember that, unless the undertaking is extremely small, you should not worry about planning every step in advance. To avoid feeling overwhelmed or trapped, begin by identifying only the initial few steps you must take, and then add more as you progress.

Set deadlines and interim goals for yourself. Setting intermediate objectives and deadlines can help you plan, be accountable, and feel more motivated to make continuous progress. You should do this if your instructor hasn't already or if they've merely set a single large target at the end.

Recognize your periods of productivity. Some pupils are more productive in the morning, whereas others are more attentive in the evening. This should be considered when planning your study and work hours for times when you are least likely to procrastinate.

Increase study motivation by becoming more motivated. You can make studying more interesting, for instance, by keeping track of the number of consecutive days you met your academic goals and rewarding yourself when the streak reaches a certain duration.

Make studying more enjoyable for students. For instance, if you feel uncomfortable studying in your room, attempt a more relaxing location, such as the library.

Create an image of yourself in the future. You could envision yourself being able to relax after completing a task, receiving commendation for a job well done, or facing the consequences of inadequate preparation.

Focus on your objectives rather than your duties. As an example, if you have tedious homework to complete, instead of focusing on the tasks, consider your academic goals and the reasons you want to do well on the assignment, such as getting a high grade in the class. Rather, consider the objective.

Clarity is the engine that drives productivity. The term 'progress' is highly relative and can only be measured in relation to a person's clearly defined objectives. What I consider to be progress may differ significantly from what you consider to be progress.

WHY?

Because these actions, regardless of how significant they may be, do not help you fulfill your life's purpose in any manner.

Therefore, you must devote as much time as possible to contemplating what is most important to you at this juncture in your life. What are the actions that, if taken, will guarantee that you are making the most of your life, given that time management is life management? Your life only progresses in the direction that time progresses.

In his book Goals: How to Get Everything You Want—Faster Than You Ever Thought Possible, Brian Tracy emphasized the significance of establishing well-defined, crystal-clear objectives.

There is a direct correlation between your level of clarity regarding who you are and what you want and virtually everything you achieve in life.

What are your aspirations for your life? What qualities do you wish to be recognized for? What are your long-, medium-, and short-term objectives? What deadlines have you set for these objectives? Who and what do you need to accomplish these objectives?

Writing down your short-term and long-term objectives is never a waste of time, but rather the first step in time management.

The more concise and straightforward your objectives are, the simpler and faster you will be able to implement them, whereas the more intricate your objectives are, the more difficult it will be to take action. You will become entirely confused about your objectives and waste time as a result.

Invest your time in writing down your thoughts, documenting your vision so that you can take immediate action and measure your progress. Get a notepad for your to-do list on which you can record your daily objectives and even affix strategies for achieving them.

In the latter portion of this book, you will learn more about how to identify tasks that you must perform personally, delegate, or, if necessary, remove from your list.

Obtain a notepad to increase your time management skills. Imagine you only have three months to live. What would you want to accomplish? Write whatever comes to mind right now as if there were no limits to what you could accomplish in three months.

2. On a new sheet, outline how you intend to attain each objective. Put your intentions on paper and visualize yourself taking action; meditate on it. Schedule time for this exercise so that you are not distracted.

Chapter 16: Our Most Valuable Currency Must Be Time.

Time Leverage
Consider the opportunity expense. This is a microeconomic theory that explains that whenever you choose to spend a resource on something, there is a risk of enduring a loss due to a missed opportunity. (Fernando, 2019) In other words, selecting one option will necessitate forgoing another possibility.

In light of this, it is evident that when you devote your time to other important aspects of your life, another opportunity will present itself, namely the chance to forego spending additional time at work. Why? Because, once again, you cannot be in two locations at once.

In saying all of this, I want you to gain knowledge of time leverage. All of these facets of your life that you'll be focusing on are equally essential, as it is difficult to choose between them. However, if you choose to do something such as sacrifice work to spend quality time with friends or family, you would want to maximize the experience. As soon as you establish the habit of maximizing every minute of your life, you will begin to see positive results in all areas of your life. In this manner, the sacrifice will always be worthwhile.

Avoid Everything That Will Induce Negativity

When you're on the path to self-transformation, you'll learn a great deal about the significance of surrounding yourself with continuously elevating and inspiring people. But this knowledge also encompasses objects, events, and the physical environment, as all of these factors influence your thoughts and emotions about things. Remember what we discussed regarding the Law of Attraction's underlying theory. In addition to being aware of your thoughts, you must remember that objects, events, and people have a significant impact on your overall outlook on life.

Because we have discussed the importance of valuing time and learning to maximize its use, you must develop the habit of not squandering time on anything that can cause you to experience negative emotions. And as soon as you allow this energy to affect you, it will have a negative effect on your thoughts, send this energy out into the universe, and cause you to receive more of the same.

Planned Pauses Can Help Reset, Refocus, and Recharge

Self-care includes taking time to recalibrate, refocus, and revitalize. While we've already discussed making a habit of activities that will help you develop confidence and self-esteem to nourish your inner being, another approach is to always center yourself.

Your confidence and self-worth have a great deal to do with the mental aspect of how you view yourself, and we know that this has a direct effect on your personal development. You cannot expect to excel in life and flourish if you have low self-esteem and lack confidence in your abilities. In order to take this a step further, we will also examine the affective aspect of self-care. This refers to how you respond to and feel about things that affect you.

This book is about mastering the fundamentals of time management. You learn to pick your battles so you don't waste your time and emotions on things that won't benefit you or that will only generate negative emotions when you learn to leverage the time you spend continually. So, when you establish a routine that will help you center yourself on a regular basis, you're taking time to reflect on past experiences and recollect yourself.

Spend Time on What Is Most Important to You

There is an obvious paradox inherent in comprehending time. On the one hand, time is infinite so long as you have oxygen in your lungs. On the other hand, time is limited when you realize that one day you will have to account for all the things you spent your time on, and at that point, nothing can be undone.

In order to establish a healthy balance in how you spend your time, it is beneficial to have a complete understanding of both sides of this situation. When time is treated as a valuable commodity, its scarcity is assumed and it is valued. However, the moment you obsess over this, you can easily fall into the trap of overthinking it, causing you to spend excessive amounts of time on fewer aspects of your life out of distress.

Spend Time Stimulating Various Senses and Emotions to Gain a Richer Life Experience

Enjoy your existence! We speak a lot about spending time with friends and family, but when we paint this picture, we typically believe that these people we care about need our time more than they need ours.

Consider the spouse who is always working and rarely home to spend time with his wife and children. If I encourage this man to spend more time with his family, we immediately envision trips and activities that will primarily benefit his children and wife. We presume that his family has a greater need for his time than he does. And this causes others to believe that gaining more from life through your various relationships benefits them more than you.

In every aspect of your life, you should be present and deliberate. Even if the man in the scenario is forced to take the children to the dog park for recreation, I will encourage him to allow himself to be stimulated and involved in the experience. This determines whether or not it is to his liking. Why? Because if you're going to devote your time to it, you should maximize it.

Slow Down

It is essential to frequently take a moment to pause and appreciate where you are in life. As aspirant individuals who are always striving to do and be better, we are perpetually preoccupied with the question, "What's next?" Immediately after completing one task, we immediately begin working on the next assignment. This keeps us on our toes and prepared for the next task.

Yes, it's important to continually challenge yourself and push yourself to be better, but sometimes you need to pause and appreciate where you are right now. This will enable you to reinforce your progression while on the path to self-discovery and success. It is sometimes very easy to go overboard in your efforts to reach the next phase of your existence.

We live in a world where external forces occasionally interfere with our intentions. Oftentimes, this can be very frustrating to deal with and can easily leave you feeling abruptly stagnant and overwhelmed by everything happening around you. When you reach this stage, further attempts to exert force may not be to your advantage. This is when it is necessary to calm down.

It is always a good idea to take a moment to reflect on where you are currently and where you've come from. In addition, it functions best when you are aware that things are not proceeding as planned or anticipated. It maintains your motivation and encourages you to believe that you are progressing, even if it isn't at the desired rate. You can routinely reinforce your progress. This may be sufficient to keep you motivated and poised, preventing you from becoming entangled in a sense of stagnation that could make you want to push or pursue further.

Utilize Time to Strive for Your Objectives
Avoid spending time inappropriately. While we may occasionally pardon 'laziness' for necessary breaks, you are not spending your time wisely if you did not initially intend to do it. You must develop the habit of consciously accounting for all of your time, even during breaks.

In every aspect of your life, you are able to express yourself to the fullest extent and be present for every experience that life has to offer if you strive to use your time judiciously and effectively.

Part 2

Three positive habits that will enrich your life

1 - Expertise in your profession or vocation

Passion is the most attractive cologne a man can wear. It is evident in his physical presence, audible in his voice, and visible in his gaze.

A man without passion is doomed to a life of mediocrity. The magnetic force that propels you toward mastery is passion.

How do I determine my genuine calling?

Focus more on competency than talent. Over time, competence will develop into mastery, which is the highest level of talent.

Even the most talented individuals must endure the arduous process of mastery.

Discovering a talent, an idea, or a purpose that inspires you and investing one's entire being in it. When mastery becomes a preoccupation, other vices take a back seat.

2 - In search of the truth

No one can fully experience the totality of existence in a single lifetime. Self-awareness is limitless. Because there is more to learn the more you learn. However, your genuine desire to uncover life's grandest truths will compel you to develop a natural discipline. Read, reflect, contemplate, investigate, and engage in novel activities... Do not be so slothful as to be satisfied with repeating someone else's remarks. Everything must be called into doubt. Seek comprehension. Introspect.

3. Command of the body and psyche

Overall health, stamina, strength, esthetic appeal, flexibility, mobility, and strength are all characteristics of a fantastic physique.

Calm, resilient, adaptable, cheerful, courageous, amusing, untainted, and devoid of mental disorders are all characteristics of a superior intellect.

In each category, at least four values must be selected. However, nothing prevents you from constructing anything!

These three "addictions" will occupy the majority of your time, attention, and energy, leaving you little time, focus, or energy to indulge in low-grade addictions...

Chapter 17: Overcoming Dependencies / Conquering Dependencies

You cannot overcome your habits unless you confront them. The more you engage in a poor habit, the more it is reinforced, and the harder it becomes to quit.

1 - Recovering from substance abuse

Discipline can be utilized to combat substance abuse. This will only work if you have an accountability partner or severe consequences for relapse. Putting your faith in your generosity or resolve is a surefire way to fail. All methods will become ineffective.

2 - Overcoming Dependence

Maturation has a natural consequence of transcendence. Similar to a child who is impotent over his toys. He spends the day with them and also spends the night with them. If you try to take them from him, he will launch a tantrum. However, as he ages, the appeal of these objects diminishes. Until one day he completely forgets about them. He will begin to view these objects as childish. When he observes other children using the same objects, he will laugh.

Similarly, as you age, you may overcome your addictions. Maturity is the product of knowledge, while consciousness is the result of comprehension. As a consequence of heightened awareness, profound insights into the whole process of temptation, indulgence, and karma will emerge. That is to say;

- why do you do it?

Self-observation is emphasized, but internal conflict is avoided. Since we've been conditioned to evaluate ourselves and others primarily in terms of "good versus evil," this is the more difficult approach. We can acquire remorse just as easily as we can acquire a new language. Unlearning and becoming accustomed to this new information takes time.

The warrior chooses the first path because he conquers himself through hard labor and resolve.

On the kingly second path, he transcends through straightforward submission.

The first path is Stoicism, while Tantra is the second.

Every expert began as a novice. Embarrassment is the cost of entry.

"Weak people have no place in this world, this life, or any other existence." The cause of slavery and other forms of suffering is frailty. Weakness is equivalent to mortality!

Avoid anything that makes you physically, mentally, or spiritually feeble. It is a toxin."

The lies you tell yourself are the most harmful because they are the most obvious.

Expose your motives, mock your justifications, and see through your foolishness...

"Assume that you do not have 10,000 years to squander. The approach of death is imminent."Do something good while you're alive if it's in your power to do so."

Poor quality self-care;

> Drinking and clubbing > Consuming expensive junk cuisine > Binge-watching television programs

Self-care to the utmost standard;

* Massage therapy * Restorative yoga * Creating art * Reading great literature * FaceTiming with family and friends * Reconnecting with nature

Create two checklists:

Exemplary men to aspire to imitate are role models.

2. Anti-models: Individuals whom you do not wish to resemble as an adult.

(In terms of reputation, lifestyle, abilities, and achievements)

Permit both lists to safeguard your lifestyle, i.e. what you do and don't do.

Socrates, Alan Watts, Bruce Lee, Naval, Aurelius, Elon Musk, Bill Gates, and Jeff Bezos are among my role models.

(Yes, I have a fascination for intelligent people who convey bare facts.)

If necessary, serve as your own coach, supporter, and therapist.

Proceed, lone predator. Make yourself valuable, and you will effortlessly attract superb clients.

Appreciate your solitude for the time being.

The majority of individuals consider idleness to be a squandering of time.

In actuality, you lose more time through your actions, as the majority of what you say and do is futile - you are merely active for the sake of activity, wasting vital energy.

It is up to you to distinguish between tasks that are essential to achieving your objective and those that are merely for the sake of bolstering your statistics.

It is crucial to remember that it is not the amount of time spent working that matters, but the amount of value provided during that time.

Stop "killing time," as you are the one who is dying each second...

Regarding physical preparation, no one has the right to be a neophyte. It is unfortunate for a man to age without appreciating the attractiveness and strength of his physique."

"When you find it difficult to get out of bed in the morning, recall yourself:

"As a human being, I have to go to work." What do I have to complain about if I'm going to accomplish the tasks I was born to accomplish? Is this what I'm supposed to do? To maintain heat by huddling under blankets?"

So you were born with the innate capacity to be "nice"? Rather than engaging in activities and gaining experience? Do you not see the vegetation, birds, ants, spiders, and bees going about their business and striving to maintain order in the world? And you are averse to fulfill your obligations as a human being? Why aren't you acting in accordance with your inclinations and nature?

You do not invest sufficient affection in yourself. You may also embrace your nature and its requirements."

"Let us prepare our minds as if the end of our lives were imminent. Let us not delay anything. Let's attempt to reconcile the books on a daily basis.Whoever spends every day completing their life never runs out of time."

"Every adversity in life is an opportunity to dig deep and utilize our inner resources. The difficulties we face may or may not teach us about our abilities. People who are prudent look beyond the immediate circumstances and strive to form the habit of applying what they have learned. Don't simply react haphazardly to an unanticipated occurrence; instead, remember to investigate what resources are available to deal with it. Perform an exhaustive investigation. You possess abilities of which you may be unaware. Search for the proper one. "Take advantage of it."

Chapter 18: Time Management Skills

Can you define time management skills?

Possessing effective time management skills incorporates a vast array of abilities. Effective time management comprises the following abilities:

Organization

If you have a system in place, keeping track of your duties and deadlines is much simpler. To be well-organized, one might take detailed, conscientious notes, keep one's space clean and orderly, and maintain an accurate calendar.

Prioritization

Determining the relative significance of your various commitments is one of the keys to effective time management. There are numerous methods for establishing priorities. In some situations, it may make sense to begin with the shorter, simpler duties and progress to the more time-consuming ones. Either you can group similar duties together or arrange them by urgency.

Communication

With practice, you can improve your communication skills and make your colleagues aware of your plans and objectives. In addition, delegation allows you to focus on the activities that will have the greatest impact on achieving your goals.

Planning

Planning is essential for time management effectiveness. Your ability to adhere to your schedule will depend on how well you have planned your meetings, duties, and day.

Delegation

Effective time management requires a singular focus on activities that advance organizational goals. Typically, managers are responsible for delegating tasks, but project management provides an excellent opportunity to refine this skill. It can be difficult to say "no" when someone asks you to do something at work, but establishing limits is essential for effective time management and productivity.

Managing Stress

Consider your emotional health as you strive to improve your time management. Effectively managing tension can keep you motivated and ensure you make the most of each day. You could accomplish this by rewarding yourself for minor accomplishments or by scheduling regular pauses throughout the day.

Investing in your development in each of these areas will help you remain at the top of your game whether you are currently employed, actively seeking work, or attempting to acquire a new skill.

Please refer to this article for twenty tips on time management for busy professionals.

Why are time management skills so significant?

The ability to organize one's duties in a manner that leads to success depends heavily on one's time management abilities. If you want to obtain a new position, you'll need to polish your application materials, conduct extensive company research, and prepare for impending interviews. You can accelerate the job search process by devoting a certain quantity of time per day to it.

If you are already employed, you may be assigned a variety of tasks to help the company accomplish its goals. Maintaining control of your schedule, meetings, and assignments is essential for your position's success.

Excellent time management enables one to be completely present and attentive. If, for example, you're late to a meeting and have to work on a project you neglected was due while others are speaking, you might miss out on information that could help you perform better on the job.

Successful time management also allows you to think creatively and take the initiative necessary to accomplish your goals. When you plan your work hours in advance, you give yourself breathing room to consider how your efforts will affect you and your organization in the grand scheme of things.

Chapter 19: Why Do We Delayed Action?

There are three obvious reasons for procrastination:

We may engage in procrastination when we are unable to manage negative emotions surrounding a task (such as fatigue, uneasiness, frailty, dissatisfaction, loathing, and self-doubt). This is especially evident when there is a 'task revolution,' perhaps because the work is exceedingly taxing or complicated. Consequently, we make every effort to avoid this inclination. To make matters worse, when we are under stress, the rational part of the mind (i.e., the prefrontal cortex) shuts down and the amygdala (the part of the brain that controls our fear response) interprets the task as a confirmed threat to our confidence or emotional health.

We accept interruptions for momentary gratification."This is precisely what makes the procrastination cycle so dreadful. The central tenet of behaviorism is that when we are rewarded for something, we tend to repeat it. Delaying a task provides assistance in the immediate present (which feels like a reward). All things considered, we continue to postpone endeavors until it becomes a consistent pattern. We submit to 'feel better' by performing an action we value.

We feel disconnected from our prospective selves.Known as the 'present disposition,' individuals are unquestionably more focused on their identity and feelings in the present. We have little concern for our future selves and make little effort to comprehend what our current decisions will mean for us in a month or two.

Chapter 20: The Importance Of Time Administration

Due to the fact that many people feel overburdened by all the demands and daily distractions, time management is crucial in today's society. This guide will provide advice on how to develop an effective routine.

Included are the benefits of being organized, the importance of prioritizing work, and being in the correct frame of mind.

This provides students with the principles and suggestions necessary to attempt to adapt to each individual's circumstances.

This will be of great interest to all professionals and employees who believe that the most effective time management skills will allow them to control their workday more efficiently and effectively, thereby increasing their productivity.

Time management is essentially personal management, which requires prioritization and execution.

We are always aware of the amount of time in a day.

We have twenty-four hours to complete all of our tasks for the day.

Therefore, we must make intelligent decisions when planning: if we fail to plan, we plan to fail.

Planning is necessary to avoid losing time due to distractions.

What we must keep in mind is that we must concentrate on the ultimate objective, which is the desired outcome.

Therefore, our emotions, energies, and actions must be aligned with the desired outcome. There ought to be no time for diversions.

Spend time relaxing and with loved ones, but keep in mind that time spent on your goals should be dedicated solely to them.

WHY IS TIME MANAGEMENT SO VITAL?

The term "time management" refers to the organization and scheduling of time spent on specific activities.

The advantages of time management are immense:

Develop a Mindset for Long-Term Achievement

Determine the High-Value Actions to Maximize Your Results and Establish Your Objectives

Prioritize Tasks in Your Time Management Strategy to Get the Right Things Done

Establish a Routine for Daily Success and Effective Goal Setting to Enhance Your Personal Effectiveness

Plan Your Time Wisely The Most Effective Way to Stop Procrastinating and Complete Your Daily To-Do List

Establishing a Plan to Break Your Long-Term Objectives Into Monthly, Weekly, and Daily Tasks

Establish a Personal, Concrete, and Strategic Action Plan Based on Your Personal and Professional Objectives

Increase Productivity to Accomplish More in Less Time Using the Most Effective Time Management Techniques

Ineffective time management can have some extremely negative consequences:

Missed deadlines Inefficiency Low quality Negative professional reputation Increased stress

Ineffective time management will destroy your productivity, which will result in missed opportunities, such as climbing the career escalator.

When you effectively manage your time, you establish a positive cycle and a success-based routine.

You will perform better at work, seize more opportunities, have more leisure time, and be happier overall.

Excellent time management skills enhance every aspect of your life dramatically. You only need to get begun!

Conclusion

Whether or not a person assigns a monetary value to their time, it is of great value. Insomnia, unhappiness, health complications, mental duress, and even premature death can result from poor time management. Most individuals are agitated by the mere thought of having insufficient time to complete their duties. And while this book discusses numerous techniques for improving time management, such as creating a calendar, setting priorities, modifying your sleeping habits, and installing productivity software, you may lack the motivation to change if you do not understand why time management is so important. Consequently, you must contemplate the big picture.

If properly applied, effective time management skills can enhance not only your professional life but also your entire life. If you maintain your professional life under control, you will have more time to focus on your personal life and relationships. And knowing that your duties and activities are on track will provide you with a sense of serenity in your personal life. Occasionally, the quality of your life improves as you feel calmer and less agitated.

In addition, another effective method for time management is to complete your most important tasks during your most productive hours. Specifically, you must determine when you are most inspired to perform. You should therefore monitor when, where, and how you are most productive. Recent research indicates that our day is governed by phenomena that influence our alertness and motivation. Before noon, for instance, you may have the most mental capacity and the most focus and attention. In the evening, you may experience a significant decline. Therefore, if you have a project that requires critical judgments and intricate thought processes, it is best to manage it during your creative hours.

Effective time management skills can have a positive impact on your work and life in general, and when you learn to take control of your time on a daily basis, you improve your ability to get things done, make better decisions, and, most importantly, acquire ultimate control over your most important responsibilities. If you have effective time management skills, your life will be vastly enhanced. The only thing left to do is implement the time management techniques discussed in this book.

www.ingramcontent.com/pod-product-compliance
Lightning Source LLC
Chambersburg PA
CBHW050234120526
44590CB00016B/2078